North Wales
Landscapes

PHOTOGRAPHS BY
Simon Kirwan

TEXT BY
Hilary Ellis

MYRIAD
LONDON

First published in 2005 by
Myriad Books Limited
35 Bishopsthorpe Road London
SE26 4PA

Photographs copyright © Simon
Kirwan
Text copyright © Hilary Ellis

ISBN 1 904 736 05 X

Designed and artwork by
Jerry Goldie Graphic Design
Printed in China

www.myriadbooks.com

Previous page: Aran Fawddwy
summit; right: Penygadair

CONTENTS

North Wales Landscapes

As a child growing up in Liverpool, we often had days out and took family holidays in North Wales, usually to the resorts of the north-west coast and to Anglesey, when the car broke down twice during the week, spent most of the holiday in a garage, and we came home by train. I remember other random events – the altar boys outing to Rhyl from St Edmund's Church, when the horse I was riding bolted.

My earliest memory of taking photographs was aged 14, lying on a grassy bank overlooking RAF Valley on Anglesey, attempting to snap Lightning jets take-off with a Kodak Vest Pocket Folding Camera, dating from 1954, which shot 120mm roll film and probably had a maximum shutter speed of 1/100th sec. The pictures were not a success.

Sitting in rain-lashed caravans in Conwy and Llandudno, I often used to draw maps of the area, copied from the *AA Book of the Road*, and I invariably became distracted by the areas on the road atlas indicating mountains. I was particularly fascinated by Carnedd Dafydd and Carnedd Llewelyn, and pictured them as Everest-like in their magnitude. Snowdon itself seemed remote and unapproachable, and certainly was not on our family agenda, which centred on drives to Betws-y-Coed to see the Swallow Falls and South Stack Lighthouse on Holy Island.

Place names began to filter into my subconscious, although I had never visited them – the Devil's Kitchen, the Nameless Cwm, the Castle of the Winds, Bristly Ridge.

Later, I spent a lot of time at a cottage on the Lleyn peninsula owned by my wife's family, and began to discover the wild character and compelling beauty of the Welsh landscape for myself. Now, visits to Wales became opportunities to venture into the mountains. We climbed Snowdon, Tryfan, the Glyders, and finally Carnedd Dafydd and Llewelyn. We discovered the further-flung reaches of Snowdonia – Cadair Idris, Aran Fawddwy, the Rhinogs. Now, instead of sitting in caravans, we had family outings on rain-lashed mountains, coaxing our children up Arenig Fawr, completing Crib Goch and the Snowdon horseshoe with my son, an outing on Tryfan's North Ridge in torrential rain, when my brother-in-law had to carry the dog down.

My career as a studio-bound photographer was at an end. I did some travelling, visiting the Alps, the Himalayas, Africa, re-discovering photography as a passion, rather than a job. I found that in the wild places of Wales, I could combine my love of the outdoors with my passion for photography. The rapid development of digital cameras meant I could carry lightweight equipment, capable of superb results. For most of the pictures in this book, I used a Fuji S2 Pro digital camera, with a variety of Sigma and Tokina lenses.

Photography can be a frustrating activity, and the time spent waiting for the light, at the right time of day and in the right place, can seem agonising. But when the clouds part, the mist clears, and the sun breaks through, the landscape is revealed in all its glory and, unpacking my camera from the rucksack, I remember once more why I am drawn back to Wales again and again.

Simon Kirwan

Left: Aran Fawddwy

NORTH SNOWDONIA

THE DOMINATING SNOWDON RANGE is at the heart of north Snowdonia – a spectacular backdrop to the coastal scenery of all north-west Wales. Over half a million visitors each year come to climb the highest and most formidable of Snowdonia's rugged ridges and summits, and to enjoy the scenery around the many beautiful lakes and valleys. Sailors travelling on ships from Ireland in the dark ages referred to the snow-covered peaks here as Snowy Hills (or *Snaudune* in Gaelic) and Snowdonia's main peaks were known as *Yr Eryri*, "the abode of the Eagles". The region is now a national park but scars of the slate industry can still be seen among the mountain crags.

MOELWYN MAWR

The slopes of Moelwyn Mawr, viewed here from the summit ridge of Cnicht, are criss-crossed with paths and scarred with evidence of northern Snowdonia's industrial heritage. Quarries and their disused tips line the sides of Cwm Croesor, where lakes and reservoirs provided water power and inclines were built to transport hard-won slate to market. From the summit of Moelwyn Mawr and Cnicht, on rain-free days, the panorama is superb with views to almost all the mountains of Snowdonia.

NANT FFRANCON PASS

The Afon Ogwen flows through the Nant Ffrancon Pass in this beautiful springtime scene. Travelling north on the A5, the rounded mounds of Foel Goch and Mynydd Perfedd to the left overlook the lush green valley. Once a lake carved by glaciers would have been found here, but it has long gone. Now the flat meadowland is a peaceful haven among the formidable peaks of the surrounding mountains.

CRIB GOCH & SNOWDON *(right and below)*

The summit of Snowdon, known as Yr Wyddfa, is the highest point in Wales at 3,560ft (1,085m). Three popular hikes ascend to its grand summit. The Llanberis Track is the easiest route but alternatives include the Pyg Track and the Miner's Track. These early morning scenes are taken from the Miner's Track, once used by men who worked on copper mines high in the mountains. One approach to Snowdon includes a daunting walk along a sharp ridge or arête via the adjoining peak of Crib Goch. Often called the "Snowdon horseshoe", this ridge and the summit of Crib Goch can be seen clearly towards the right of this photograph, dominating the view of Llyn Llydaw in the foreground. Below, Glaslyn lies under Snowdon's pyramidal peak.

LLYN LLYDAW *(below)*

On Snowdon's eastern flank lies Llyn Llydaw, the Welsh claimant to the home of the Lady of the Lake, famous from Arthurian legend as the keeper of the sword Excalibur. Sir Bedivere is reputed to have thrown Excalibur into the lake after King Arthur's death. The lake lies at over 1,400ft (427m) and pipes from the lake feed water to the Cwm Dyli hydroelectric power station almost 1,000 ft (300m) below. Copper ore from the Glaslyn mine was once crushed on the shore and the water has a greenish hue. Vestiges of copper mining can be seen along the route of the Miner's Track, which passes over a causeway on the lake constructed in 1853. Until then, ore carts were loaded onto rafts for the lake crossing.

CRIB GOCH *(above)*

The rocks and crags of Crib Goch tower above the freezing waters of Llyn Llydaw in this arresting scene. An ascent to the ridge of Crib Goch can be extremely dangerous in winter and requires proper equipment. But a climb to Llyn Llydaw, for views of the Snowdon horseshoe, can be most enjoyable when the track is free of the crowds that climb in summer. All around is evidence of a great glacier that swept down from Snowdon to the valley of Cwm Dyli.

LLYN TEYRN *(right)*

Further down the Miner's Track from Llyn Llydaw lies a small corrie lake, Llyn Teyrn. The well-worn track winds around the lake with fabulous views back to Snowdon and the ridge to Y Lliwedd. Buildings beside the lake are the remains of miners' barracks for the local copper mines. *Teyrn* means monarch and most probably refers to King Arthur; many Arthurian legends are associated with locations around Snowdon.

NANTGWYNANT PASS *(right)*

This beautiful wintry photograph overlooks the peaceful Nantgwynant valley from a viewpoint on the A498 to Beddgelert. Beneath the towering peaks of the Snowdon horseshoe, the pipeline carrying water from Llyn Llydaw can be seen clearly on the mountainside. Built in 1905, the Cwm Dyli hydroelectric power station is one of the oldest running in the UK today, with a single generator producing electricity for the National Grid.

ROYAL BRIDGE (left)

The view of the Snowdon peaks from Royal Bridge, near Capel Curig, is one of the most attractive in Wales and much favoured by photographers and painters. In this almost-Alpine setting are all the elements that combine to create a perfect scene in northern Snowdonia: the still and glassy blue waters of the lake are backed by dramatic distant mountains on the horizon. The snow cover and gleaming afternoon sunlight add to the romantic effect and there is a feeling of being surrounded by silence and privy to secret and unspoilt views. Here is a place to admire Snowdon without effort.

TRYFAN

The intimidating crags of Tryfan are the haunt of mountain climbers who relish the challenge of the rugged rocks and deathly drops. To reach the summit requires some scrambling, and in icy, wet or windy weather conditions Tryfan can be a dangerous place. Those who train to climb Mount Everest favour Tryfan's exposed slabs and buttresses and further crags around the Glyders. The hike to the summit is just six miles long, but ascends sharply, reaching 3,000ft (915m) after a strenuous effort. The three stone buttresses that can be seen on the peak's east face have given Tryfan its name.

LLYN IDWAL

Located in arguably the most dramatic cwm in North Wales, Llyn Idwal is cradled by the three craggy peaks of Glyder Fawr, Twll Du and Y Garn. This footbridge at the lake's edge looks towards Y Gribin, a ridge extending from between the Glyders. Cwm Idwal is a nature reserve and the shallow cirque lake has unusually rich plant life and plenty of fish. It is also rich in legend. A moraine on the lake's western shore is said to be the burial place of the giant, Idwal. It is also said that no bird flies over the lake's surface, and that a wailing voice can be heard when there is a storm in the cwm.

CWM IDWAL WITH TRYFAN AND GLYDERS BEHIND

Cwm Idwal is also the most accessible cwm in Britain, just a short distance from one of the busiest roads in Wales. The nature reserve was the first to be established in Wales in 1954, and uses enclosures to explore the effect of sheep and goats grazing on the rich plant life. Heather and purple moor grass grows at the northern end of the lake, while at the southern end, where the lake becomes a stream with small waterfalls, sub-Arctic flora grows alongside tufted hair grass and yarrow. The cwm has attracted botanists, anglers, geologists and climbers for many years.

LLYN PADARN & THE SNOWDON RANGE

(above and right)

These attractive photographs show Llyn Padarn's most spectacular view: looking towards the famous Llanberis Pass with the Snowdon range's northern flank majestic in the afternoon sunlight. The lake is two miles long and situated in a wide glacial valley. On the lake's southern shore is Llanberis, from where the Snowdon Mountain Railway carries tourists to its summit by a five-mile scenic route. The entire valley is strewn with boulders, while hillside oak woodland and the Dinorwic slate quarries overlook the lake.

LLYN PADARN *(above and right)*

During the industrial age, Llyn Padarn was a
commercial waterway, transporting ore from the
copper mines around Nant Peris to Cwm-y-glo. It
was not until 1830 that a road was built by the mining
companies, enabling them to transport ore from
Pen-y-Pass to Caernarfon more effectively. Today the
lake is a scenic spot, and the site of the Llyn Padarn
Country Park. Boats are available for hire, and the lake
is a popular spot for canoeing, windsurfing and sailing.
It is also popular with anglers and boasts excellent
brown trout fishing in season.

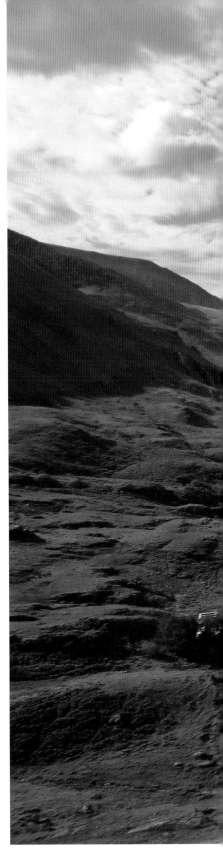

LLANBERIS PASS *(left)*

The Afon Nant Peris runs along the length of the rugged Llanberis Pass, beside the pass road built in the early 19th century by the local mining companies. Among scree and rocky debris, the stream grows bigger as it is joined by others that tumble from the lofty heights of the Glyders and the Snowdon range. Climbers flock to Pen-y-Pass, the highest starting point for hikes to the Snowdon horseshoe.

NANT FFRANCON PASS *(above)*

The desolate wilderness of the Nant Ffrancon Pass is here viewed from the south, at the edge of Llyn Ogwen. The green valley is sandwiched between the Carneddau to the right and the Glyderau to the left, and levels out towards Bethesda. Before Thomas Telford's A5 route was carved from the valley sides, slate was transported along a route through the pass known as the most dreadful horse path in Wales.

PEN YR OLE WEN & OGWEN COTTAGE

The path to Cwm Idwal starts at Ogwen Cottage, beside Llyn Ogwen and close to waterfalls on the Afon Ogwen. The scene is overlooked by the dark brow of Pen yr Ole Wen, a major mountain at the foot of the Carneddau range. Its steadily rising slope and crag-free south face makes it difficult to judge its enormous size, over 200ft (60m) higher than Tryfan across the pass. It is a relentless climb to the summit, with much scrambling across rock, but splendid panoramic views include breathtaking sights of the Menai Strait, Anglesey, Snowdon, the Glyders, Tryfan and the Carneddau.

PEN YR OLE WEN AND CWM IDWAL *(above)*

Clouds cast shadows on the soft and marshy ground that walkers must cross to reach the summit ridge of Pen yr Ole Wen.
This aspect from beside Cwm Idwal, 1,220ft (370m) above sea level, towards Pen yr Ole Wen and the southerly mountains of the
Carneddau range, is dramatic and geologically ancient. Charles Darwin and Professor Adam Sedgwick (widely regarded as the father
of modern geology) visited Cwm Idwal in 1831 and examined rocks for fossils. Sedgwick did not believe that glaciers had any effect
in shaping the landscape and so both scientists failed to spot the generous glacial evidence. Darwin later wrote that a house burnt
down by fire could not have told its story more plainly than Cwm Idwal, but Sedgwick continued to refute the theory until his
death 42 years after their visit.

DISUSED QUARRY BELOW FOEL DDU

Slate-quarrying remains line the flanks of Cwm Croesor, just two miles from the slate capital of North Wales, Blaenau Ffestiniog. The Rhosydd Slate Quarry, under the shadow of Foel Ddu, quarried an estimated 220 million slates in its 80 year history. In one of the wettest parts of North Wales, slateworkers toiled both above and below ground, quarrying deeper with the years. At its peak in the 1880s, 200 workers mined 6,000 tons of saleable slate each year. Quarrymen would hike to barracks each Monday morning with enough food for the week. Rhosydd was notorious for its crowded and damp barracks and the worst living conditions in the industry.

DISUSED QUARRY BELOW FOEL DDU

The evocative remains of the quarrymen's barracks still stand, although the mills were
demolished in the 1940s for the slate in their walls. Underground mining took place in
candlelight and eventually reached a depth of 14 floors, most of which are now flooded.
In the early days, slate was transported to the Afon Dwyryd near Maentwrog by packhorse,
but in 1864 a link was made to the Croesor Tramway, leading directly to Porthmadog.

CNICHT SUMMIT LOOKING WEST TO THE SNOWDON RANGE

Majestic views of Snowdon and Crib Goch, beyond the fine valley of Nantgwynant, can be seen from the sharp and rocky summit of Cnicht. At 2,260ft (689m), the climb from Croesor is deceptively easy to start with and ends in a scramble, dangerous in this often wet and windy landscape. Views to the right of the Snowdon range reveal the Glyders, and to the left, the Hebogs. From roads to the south-west of Cnicht, the mountain appears pyramidal and has been called the Welsh Matterhorn. In fact the summit is on a fine ridge, and the pointed peak is a cross section of the mountain. The mountain range on which Cnicht stands stretches to the east where it ends at Moel Siabod; both are sometimes referred to as "the book ends".

CNICHT *(above and top right)*

Looking south-west along the ridge from the summit of Cnicht are wonderful views of the Glaslyn Estuary (Traeth Bach).
Behind the estuary lie the rugged Rhinog mountains, dotted with lakes and woodland. To the west are grand views of
Cardigan Bay and the Lleyn peninsula. From the summit of Cnicht, and of the Moelwyn mountains to the south, steam
trains of the Ffestiniog Railway can be heard as they curve and wind their way along the Vale of Ffestiniog to Porthmadog.

CNICHT (below)

On the descent from Cnicht, beyond the disused quarries at Bwlch Cwmorthin, the path reaches the picturesque glaciated valley of Cwm Croesor. The summit of Cnicht lies on the north side of the valley where its rocky sides meet the grassy lower slopes. The valley was once alive with the hum and activity of slate quarrying but is now a quiet, beautiful backwater. There are many industrial relics along the way, and the path meets the route of the railway that once carried slates to Porthmadog.

CWM CORSIOG & LLYN CWM-CORSIOG

Beyond the ridge of Cnicht and past the wild and remote Llyn y Biswail is Cwm Corsiog. This treeless valley is the first evidence of the slate industry on the route from Croesor. The large lake to the left, Llyn Cwm-corsiog, is purely artificial, created to supply water power for the mine workings. In all, 12 reservoirs supplied water for the Rhosydd Slate Quarry and abundant rain kept the lakes topped up. But during drought, or freezing winter weather, production ground to a halt.

MOELWYN MAWR

The rocky underfoot of Cnicht's summit is the striking foreground for a view of Moelwyn Mawr, under clouds that stretch into the distant yonder. Moelwyn Mawr is some 265ft (81m) higher than Cnicht and its grassy slopes bear the scars of the slate industry. Its adjoining peak, Moelwyn Bach, is a rockier climb and from the summit there are views to the coast and, in good visibility, Criccieth Castle. Both Moelwyns overlook a dam at Llyn Stwlan, which feeds the Tanygrisiau hydroelectric power station.

LLYN CWM-CORSIOG

Created in 1889, Llyn Cwm-corsiog is impounded by two dams by the quarryside at Bwlch Cwmorthin. Other lakes in the area were enlarged by the quarrying companies for further water. Much of the power harnessed was used to operate pumps that kept the underground workings dry and accessible in wet weather. Water power was also used to operate slate-dressing machines and to power the inclines that linked the quarries to the Croesor Tramway.

Llyn Peris & Afon Rhythallt at Pen-y-Llyn

Adjoining Llyn Padarn is the smaller, but equally picturesque Llyn Peris, with impressive views towards the Llanberis Pass and its surrounding mountains. Sadly, much waste from the Dinorwic slate quarries was tipped by the lake's eastern shore and tourists crowd more readily to Llyn Padarn's waterfront. Beyond the Llanberis Lake Railway's northernmost point on Llyn Padarn lies the Pont Pen-y-Llyn, a bridge that marks the site where Llyn Padarn ends and the lake becomes a river. The river winds its way to the coast at Caernarfon, first as Afon Rhythallt and then as the more famous Afon Seiont.

LLANBERIS AND SNOWDON

This idyllic late afternoon scene captures the true magic of Snowdonia in spring. Fine tufts of grass appear to flicker
in the wind, beside heather and stray boulders patterned with lichen. Shadows on the sides of Snowdon add definition
to the many ridges and valleys carved by glaciers in the Ice Age. Llanberis sits among thick forest at the foot of the
mountain, beside a lake of striking blue. Mining is out of sight, but Llanberis developed entirely to support the industry,
with slate mined at Dinorwic and copper mined on Snowdon's slopes. When mining came to an end, the village focused
its energies on tourism. An ideal base for climbs to Snowdon's summit, both on foot and by train, the lake is also a
magnet for anglers and watersports enthusiasts. The region's heritage is recorded in the Welsh Slate Museum.

LLYN OGWEN & TRYFAN *(left)*

The towering crags of Tryfan stand alongside Llyn Ogwen in this magnificent photograph of bare mountain scenery. Llyn Ogwen is almost 990ft (300m) above sea level and one of the shallowest lakes in the area – an average of just 6ft (1.8m) deep. And yet trout thrive in its light blue waters. Around the lake, along an old fisherman's path, are grand views of Tryfan's giant buttresses, including the Milestone Buttress, one of the earliest crags to attract climbers.

Y GARN FROM CWM IDWAL *(below)*

To Cwm Idwal's western end is Y Garn, one of three rocky crags around the lake. Crumbling ledges support rare flora, while thick slabs and walls of rock present satisfying challenges for climbers. Cwm Idwal was named by the 12th-century prince, Owain Gwynedd, for his son Idwal. Owain's vain cousin, Nefydd, had been entrusted with Idwal's care but was jealous of his scholarship and good looks. Nefydd arranged for his son, Dunawd, to push Idwal in the lake where he drowned.

IDWAL SLABS & GLYDER FAWR *(above)*

The gentle incline of the famous Idwal slabs is immeasurably deceptive. Though rock climbers visit these rocks in their thousands each week during summertime, not one of the many routes is easy. Three of the most famous are known as Faith, Hope and Charity. Glyder Fawr, the highest mountain in the range, is a magnificent backdrop to this scene.

BRISTLY RIDGE & GLYDER FACH *(right)*

It is a good scramble up the Bristly ridge from Bwlch Tryfan, though the pinnacled ridge looks daunting from below. There is an alternative route up a scree path, but both lead to a prominent pile of rocks on which the overhanging "cantilever" rock is settled. Beyond it, an enormous collection of slabs and boulders marks the summit of Glyder Fach.

CWM IDWAL & GLYDERS *(above)*

The Afon Clyd flows beside the path between Cwm Idwal and Llyn Ogwen. Some of the pebbles in the lake and river contain fossils of trilobytes and brachiopods, buried in sedimentary marine deposits and volcanic ash 450 million years ago and brought to the surface by the earth's movements. The downwash of loose morainic material from the higher slopes has strewn rocks and boulders across the valley, and the river courses over them. In some areas, the grass is rich and green from the minerals and soil deposits of the glacier. Cwm Idwal is the most southerly place in Britain to see plants common in glacial environments. In the peat surrounding the lake is evidence of ancient birch trees, though the area is now treeless.

CASTELL Y GWYNT, GLYDER FACH & GLYDER FAWR

SUMMIT *(right and below)*
The striking collection of stones on Glyder Fach is known enchantingly as Castell y Gwynt, or Castle of the Winds, after the singing sound created when strong winds blow through the hollows in a certain direction. The vertical masses of slate are encountered when traversing the broad ridge between the Glyders. There are many on Glyder Fawr's summit, as well as breathtaking views of Snowdon across the Llanberis Pass.

ICE PINNACLES ON CARNEDD LLEWELYN

On a crisp winter's day the scenery in Snowdonia can be magnificent. In this dramatic photograph ice pinnacles are encountered on the ridge between Carnedd Llewelyn, the third highest Welsh peak, and its neighbour Yr Elen. Looking south, the mountains that rise to the Glyders can be seen and the sun casts striking shadows.

WATERFALL, OGWEN VALLEY WITH TRYFAN BEHIND

Waters from Llyn Ogwen tumble down to the valley floor of the Nant Ffrancon Pass at Rhaeadr Ogwen (Ogwen Falls). These mighty falls are amongst the best known in Snowdonia. The stone bridge, Pont Pen-y-benglog, stands under the shadow of Tryfan and the Glyders in this picturesque and springtime scene. Beneath the arch of the bridge is an older bridge, possibly built by the Romans.

VALE OF CLWYD

The Vale of Clwyd's distinctive low valley floor is patterned with a patchwork of snow-covered grassy fields in this tranquil scene. The vale is bounded by the Clwydian Range behind and the more gentle hills of the Denbighshire uplands ahead. Snowdonia lies beyond on the horizon. The valley here runs for about 30km (18 miles) from Ruthin to the coast at Rhyl. Archaeological finds suggest that this rich agricultural land was occupied in 6000 BC, and Iron Age hill forts stand on the Clwydian Hills. Walks in these hills are more gentle with views of the medieval market towns at Ruthin and Denbigh. Both towns stand by the ruins of once-mighty castles, and are surrounded by well-preserved town defences.

SWALLOW FALLS

In the heart of Snowdonia, to the west of Betws-y-Coed, are views of the magnificent Swallow Falls. The waterfall is especially spectacular after heavy rains when water charges down among the rocks in a deafening roar. Easily accessed from beside Thomas Telford's famous road, now known as the A5, Swallow Falls is a popular stopping point for those exploring the valleys and peaks of the region. Also known as Rhaeadr Ewynnol, the English name comes from a mistranslation of the Welsh – the word "ewynnol" meaning frothy was mistaken for "wennol", the Welsh for swallow. It is the highest continuous waterfall in Wales, and lies on the Afon Llugwy, a trout and salmon-filled river that flows through beautiful wooded glens.

CONWY MOUNTAIN FROM TOP OF SYCHNANT PASS *(right)*

The foothills of the mighty Carneddau mountain range stretch far north to Conwy, meeting the coast at Conwy Bay. Here lies Conwy Mountain (Mynydd y Dref), an easy climb with wonderful coastal outlooks. Its proximity to Conwy ensures that the mountain is always busy with walkers enjoying the fresh air and hiking on one of its many paths. In this photograph, a family walks on the mountain's south-side beside a drop towards the Sychnant Pass, the inland route connecting Conwy and Penmaenmawr. Regarded by many travellers as dangerous, the main road now passes through tunnels along the coast.

WILD PONIES ON CONWY MOUNTAIN

Two wild ponies roam freely amongst the bracken and ponds on Conwy Mountain. There are fewer than 300 semi-wild ponies living on the Carneddau range and they are the surprise and delight of many hikers in the region. Legend suggests that the wild ponies give birth to their foals under the cliffs of Yr Elen, but there are miles of mountains to explore. Though Snowdonia is famous for the overwhelming dominance of its sheep population, it is also home to a wide range of wild mammals, from feral goats that climb the hillsides of Tryfan to pine martens, polecats and otters.

Moel Siabod

The graceful peak of Moel Siabod (2861ft/872m) is the first mountain that many visitors will see as they enter Snowdonia National Park from Betws-y-Coed. At the foot of the mountain's eastern flanks lies Llyn y Foel. Behind it is the rough ridge that must be climbed to reach the top. From the rocky summit cairn are fine views over the sheer drop to Llynau Mymbyr and the cwm below. Under low and brooding clouds is a magnificent panorama, looking into the heart of Snowdonia, with the Snowdon horseshoe beautifully defined.

NORTH-WEST COAST

THE NORTH-WEST COAST of Wales takes in an array of scenic beauty including Anglesey and the thin finger of the Lleyn peninsula. Sandy bays and rocky coves line the cliff-backed coastlines. While the land is relatively low-lying, it is often backed dramatically by views of the Snowdonia mountains. Though remote, both the Lleyn peninsula and Anglesey are increasingly popular with holidaymakers seeking surf and sail. But history permeates at all levels, from the dramatic Victorian bridges that tower over the Menai Strait and spectacular Edwardian castles at Beaumaris, Conwy and Caernarfon, to stories of shipwrecks, Arthurian battles and the progress of Christian pilgrims. Colours are vivid, with green and fertile fields, brilliant blue bays, golden beaches and spectacular summer sunsets of all shades.

MENAI BRIDGE

The Menai Suspension Bridge towers over the Menai Strait and separates the North Wales mainland from the Isle of Anglesey. Viewed from Church Island, the colours of the bridge and scenery are pronounced by the evening sunlight, while the foothills of Snowdonia are clearly visible. Designed by Thomas Telford and completed in 1826, a clearance of 100ft (30m) was required so that tall sailing ships could continue to travel along the Strait. The bridge was just one of many challenges Telford faced in improving the London to Holyhead route, essential for crossings to Ireland.

BENLLECH

The popular seaside resort of Benllech is famous for its fine golden sands and safe, blue waters which are ideal for paddling and bathing. Set in a crescent-shaped bay and surrounded by fossil-studded cliffs, the low tide reveals miles of beautiful beach. Walks from Benllech along the cliffs are ideal for nature lovers, with birdwatching particularly good. The area is rich in ancient history: a neolithic burial chamber and the remains of 4th-century huts are close by, whilst the grave of a Viking was found in 1945 on a sandy ridge facing Benllech Sands.

CONWY

The estuary at Conwy is dominated by Edward I's dark-stoned medieval castle and crossed by three parallel bridges. This photograph shows a clear view of Robert Stephenson's tubular railway bridge. Note the mock fortifications designed for each exit, allowing the bridge to blend in with its surroundings. Behind it are two further bridges for road traffic including a suspension bridge designed by Telford. The castle itself was constructed within four years and was a key fortress in Edward's fearsome "iron ring" of castles built to subdue the Welsh.

CONWY MOUNTAIN

At just over 800ft (240m) high, Conwy Mountain's peak is reached by clear-to-follow paths and a relatively easy climb. The mountain is criss-crossed with tracks and covered with bracken and gorse. At the summit are magnificent panoramic views of Conwy and its estuary, Llandudno, Snowdonia and the Menai Strait. Its proximity to Conwy has made this climb one of the most popular in Wales, and a return journey can take in the site of an Iron Age fort (Castell Caer Leion) and the attractive Sychnant Pass (Bwlch Sychnant) with superb views of Anglesey.

CONWY ESTUARY

Today the blue waters of the harbour at Conwy are busy with yachts and pleasure craft but it was once a bustling port, shipping slate from Blaenau Ffestiniog around the world. The main industry for many years was mussel-gathering, and a pearl found during the reign of Charles II adorns the crown jewels. In 1991 the world's first immersed tube tunnel was constructed underneath the estuary at Conwy, allowing traffic on its way to Holyhead (and ultimately Dublin) to by-pass the town, reducing congestion over Conwy's three bridges and through the medieval walled town.

BEAUMARIS CASTLE *(above)*

Beaumaris was the last and largest of the castles built by Edward I to restrain the Welsh and construction was never fully completed. The castle was designed by Edward's favourite architect, Master James of St George, with almost geometric symmetry and is an example of a true concentric castle. The 18ft (5.5m) wide moat can still be seen around some parts of the castle.

BEAUMARIS COURTHOUSE *(right)*

Opposite the castle stands the whitewashed Beaumaris courthouse, built in 1614. Some of Anglesey's most notorious criminals stood in the dock here including the Crigyll robbers. For over 30 years this gang lured ships onto the Crigyll rocks using beacons and lights, then plundered the wrecks. The robbers included respected members of the community and they proved extremely difficult to convict.

BEAUMARIS PIER AND TOWN CENTRE *(above and left)*

The picturesque 13th-century town is filled with brightly coloured antique shops and lively pubs, cafes and restaurants. The rambling mixture of medieval, Georgian, Victorian and Edwardian architecture gives Beaumaris a unique charm. There are breathtaking views of Snowdonia across the tidal Menai Strait and plenty of opportunities for fishing and sailing on cruises from the pier.

Until the 1950s, many thousands of tourists arrived in North Wales on paddle steamers from Liverpool. Some of the most popular routes stopped at Beaumaris pier on their way down the Menai Strait to Caernarfon. A landing stage and pavilion on the pier became unsafe after lack of maintenance and were demolished, but regular repair work has prevented any further deterioration.

BEAUMARIS SEAFRONT *(above and below)*

The terraced Regency houses on the seafront are beautifully painted in pastel shades and are reminiscent of the seafront housing in Brighton and other towns on England's southern coast. Beaumaris was known as Rhosfair and Barnover, but named Beaumaris by Edward I from the French for "beautiful marsh". The castle itself was erected on low ground so that vessels might unload under its walls and the town grew up beside the castle as an administrative port and market town.

Visitors to Beaumaris can wander the narrow streets and admire the buildings, as well as explore the courthouse, Victorian gaol and toy museum. A tribute to family games and play over the last 150 years, the Museum of Childhood Memories contains over 2,000 exhibits in nine cosy rooms from tinplate toys to doll's houses and nursery furniture.

LAVAN SANDS *(above)*

Coastal walks between Beaumaris and Penmon are largely determined by the tide. Picking your way along the foreshore among the rocks and seaweed gives views of the mainland across the Lavan Sands (Traeth Lafan). Before the Menai Suspension Bridge was built, ferries took passengers across the Strait here from Bangor to Beaumaris pier. The fast-moving tides often made this journey treacherous, and many boats capsized or ran aground.

YNYS MOELFRE

To the north of the town of Moelfre, across
the narrow channel of Y Swnt, lies Ynys
Moelfre, a small outcrop inhabited by seagulls
and cormorants. In the distance are striking
views of Snowdonia. These shallow waters have
seen some of Moelfre's most challenging sea
rescues including that of the *Hindlea*, a light
coaster which, while at anchor, was dragged by
hurricane force winds perilously close to the
shore in October, 1959. The local lifeboat made
10 heroic journeys to the ship, managing to save
all eight members on board.

MOELFRE BEACH

Moelfre is an idyllic seaside resort on Anglesey's
north coast. The seafront is an excellent vantage
point for spotting ocean-going and coastal
vessels sailing to and from Merseyside. In
adverse weather conditions, these vessels
sometimes shelter in the bay. Boat trips from
Moelfre offer an opportunity to explore the
diverse wildlife along this shipwreck coast, and
visit the nearby seal colony at Ynys Dulas.

MOELFRE BOATHOUSE

This view of Moelfre's boathouse and slipway shows a calm and quiet sea, but the Moelfre lifeboat crew have been involved in many heroic rescues in strong winds, earning scores of medals for bravery. A lifeboat station was established at Moelfre in 1830, whilst this boathouse and slipway were constructed in 1909. The history of Moelfre's lifeboats is recorded on the inner walls of the lifeboat house and in a local museum.

PORTH YR YNYS

Known also as Swnt, the beach of Porth yr Ynys is backed by picturesque cottages and looks over the sound to Ynys Moelfre. The coastline in this area is rich in wildflowers such as ragwort, sea campion and thrift, which grow in abundance alongside the rocks and shingle of the shore. Bottle-nosed dolphins can occasionally be seen diving around the waters close to the island.

PENMON

The rocks of the Penmon peninsula, located at the eastern tip of Anglesey, have been quarried for centuries and used in the construction of roads and castles, including nearby Beaumaris Castle. This dramatic photograph shows limestone rubble revealed by a low tide, while Puffin Island lies across a deceptively calm stretch of water. Also known as Priestholm or Ynys Seiriol, the island became a religious settlement in the 6th century and ruins of medieval monastic buildings are found there.

PENMON PRIORY

The roofless refectory forms part of the priory at Penmon, much of which still stands today. Though a monastery was founded in the 6th century, and a wooden building constructed in the 10th century, it is the church building constructed from stone in the 12th century that remains. The priory survived the Edwardian conquest and was dissolved in the 16th century. The priory church, much of which was reconstructed in the 19th century, remains in use today.

CEMAES BAY, HARBOUR *(above and right)*

The natural, sheltered harbour of Cemaes Bay has become a centre for maritime activities. Classed as an Area of Outstanding Beauty, many of the bay's cliffs and beaches are owned by the National Trust. Sunsets over the bay are superb, and the changing seas and skies are popular with artists. Cemaes looks north to the Irish Sea and is the most northerly village in Wales. The harbour was formerly constructed in the early 19th century, when a small stone pier was added by local fishermen. After it was destroyed by a fierce storm in 1828, a new pier designed by a local entrepreneur was built. Shipbuilding took place in Cemaes, which for many years was the principal port on the north coast for trade in coal and stone. Mining activities on Parys Mountain led to the extension of the harbour, and to the development of nearby Amlwch Port.

CEMAES BAY

Cemaes has two beaches, Traeth Mawr and Traeth Bach, which are separated by the stone harbour and the River Wygyr. Both beaches have a gentle slope and are popular with families and children. The larger beach, Traeth Mawr, has rockpools to explore, and further round the bay are more isolated beaches. Boat trips can be taken from the harbour to many parts of Anglesey.

CEMLYN BAY, CLIFF VIEWS *(above and right)*

On Anglesey's north coast lies Cemlyn Bay, a two-mile stretch of coastline owned by the National Trust. On calm days such as this, cliff views can stretch to the Isle of Man. A saltwater lagoon here is run as a wildlife sanctuary. Cut off from the sea by a storm-driven shingle spit, the site is a haven for waders and seabirds. Many maritime plants including sea-kale grow on the headlands.

CEMLYN BAY, LIFEBOAT MEMORIAL *(below)*

On the headland, Trwyn Cemlyn, is a prominent memorial stone commemorating the launch of Anglesey's first lifeboat in 1828. The Reverend James Williams of Llanfair-yn-Nghornwy and his wife, Frances, founded the Anglesey Association for the Preservation of Life from Shipwrecks, following the sinking of a sailing ship and loss of all 140 on board. The RNLI took over the association's work in 1885 and still protects life at sea around Anglesey today.

THE SKERRIES *(right)*

At sunset, views of The Skerries and its famous lighthouse can be spectacular. Two miles off Carmel Head, on the north-west coast of Anglesey, this group of treeless, jagged rocks was a sailing blackspot for hundreds of years. A light was proposed as early as 1658, and the lighthouse's construction in the early 18th century made the isolated outcrop home to brave lighthouse-keepers for over 270 years. The lighthouse is now fully automated and was recently restored.

BULL BAY *(below)*

The rugged, rocky cove of Bull Bay (Porth Llechog) is a quiet and pleasant spot overlooked by hotels and a golf course. The bay has some beautiful cliff walks and the area is popular with fishermen and yachtsmen, when weather and tide permit. The English name, Bull Bay, is thought to be derived from the name of a pool on the beach, "Pwll y Tarw" or the Bull's Pool.

BENLLECH *(right)*
Families enjoy the summer sun on the magnificent wide sands of Benllech beach. In this view from the northern end of the beach, the Penmon headland can be seen stretching into the distance. Beyond it lies Great Orme on the mainland, while clouds obscure the mountains of Snowdonia. At low tide it is possible for faster walkers to reach the Penmon headland by traversing three miles of soft sands in Red Wharf Bay.

ANGLESEY SUNSET ACROSS MENAI STRAIT

The currents of the Menai Strait rush rapidly over bedrock and boulders in many parts and travel slowly in others, depositing mud and sand to create a rich environment for over 1,000 species of marine plants and animals. This dramatic sunset at low tide casts a pearly glow on deceptively calm waters. Changing tides in the channel can cause the water to swirl in different directions.

RED WHARF BAY

On the east coast, Red Wharf Bay or Traeth Coch is the largest beach on Anglesey at low tide, but at high tide it is a lengthy five-mile walk around its muddy saltmarsh shores and sand dunes. As well as several small rock pools, the bay attracts a large number of waterfowl and wading birds including curlew, oystercatchers, purple sandpipers and grey plover.

CRICCIETH

(above and right)

The castle at Criccieth stands high
on an outcrop of green felsite rock.
Reached by a steep climb, the castle
was originally built by the Welsh but
was ruined by fire after changing hands
several times. It has now been restored
and a museum on site explains its
history. Criccieth is known as "the pearl
of Wales on the shore of Snowdonia"
and is most famous for its associations
with David Lloyd George, the Liberal
statesman and prime minister who
grew up nearby and addressed crowds
at political meetings in Market Square.
Criccieth's two beaches, with safe
swimming and bathing, are often
visited by porpoises.

CAERNARFON

Boats moor in Caernarfon harbour, overlooked by the grand presence of Caernarfon castle's polygonal towers and curtain walls. One of Edward I's many military strongholds, the castle was positioned on a peninsula at the foot of the Menai Strait where Norman and Roman fortifications had once stood. The castle's design was inspired by the Roman city of Constantinople and the Eagle Tower, seen to the left, was crowned with stone eagles as a symbol of imperial power. Edward's son was born in the castle and became the first English Prince of Wales in 1301. In the 20th century, both Edward VIII and Prince Charles became Princes of Wales in controversial investiture ceremonies held in the castle. Four thousand guests attended Prince Charles' investiture, and a television audience of 500 million viewers watched the event.

ABERSOCH HARBOUR *(below)*

Wide bays and rocky coves lie between dramatic mountain cliffs on the beautiful Lleyn peninsula. The climate is unusually mild, attracting holidaymakers to Lleyn's sandy beaches and windy headlands. Sailing is the most popular pastime for many visitors to the coast here. Abersoch, on the south side of the peninsula, is known across North Wales for its yachting and sailing. The natural harbour and sandbanks stretch for two to three miles into Tremadog Bay, and the flat waters are ideal for watersports enthusiasts. Fishing is also plentiful, and regular trips from Abersoch head out to the waters around the St Tudwal islands for mackerel fishing, and to view caves and seabirds.

PWLLHELI

(above and right)

Hundreds of yachts are berthed in the large marina at Pwllheli, the unofficial capital and market town of the Lleyn peninsula. Facilities for sailing are excellent. Pwllheli was once an important centre for ship-building and sea trade but today the harbour is almost landlocked. The gradual build-up of sand in the harbour, and the decline of sea trading in the area, led to Pwllheli's reinvention as a holiday town. The railway brought tourists from industrial areas to recreational spots including a seafront promenade and Butlin's holiday camp.

ABERSOCH SAILING *(above and right)*
In Manchester's bid to hold the 2000 Olympics, Abersoch was named as the intended site for sailing competitions. The sandy beaches give way to choppy and challenging seas, making Abersoch an obvious spot to launch any seagoing craft. The popularity of sailing in the area has meant that recovery facilities are of the highest calibre and regular events for all watersports are held. The relatively sheltered conditions in the bay are ideal for learning and recreational sailing, while the more challenging conditions offshore are set against the magnificent backdrop of Snowdonia. The harbour, straddling the Afon Soch, is a pleasant place to sit and watch crafts come and go.

ABERSOCH BEACHES

Horse-riding along the beach is just one of many ways to enjoy outdoor pursuits in Abersoch. Almost too successful, the town is hugely crowded at peak season and its three beaches are full of activity. The northernmost beach, known as The Warren, or Quarry beach, has good sand at low tide that stretches to the rocky headland of Trwyn Llanbedrog. Cliffs here reach up towards the mountain, Mynydd Tir-y-Cwmwd, which at 433ft (132m) has wonderful panoramic views that take in the great expanse of Cardigan Bay. Footpaths zigzag the heather and gorse-covered headland, which is topped by a tin man sculpture that can be seen from the beach at Llanbedrog.

ABERSOCH ACTIVITIES

Thrill-seekers of all kinds descend on Abersoch for events throughout the year. In summer, the main beach is always busy with activity. International events and national championships are held here, from extreme sports such as wakeboarding and Zapcat racing to longboat challenges, dinghy racing and regattas. The main beach is protected from prevailing winds and is ideal for windsurfing, waterskiing, sailing and powerboating. Not to mention simply relaxing on the shore and taking in the views of St Tudwal's Islands.

BEACH HUTS, ABERSOCH

The annual regatta at Abersoch includes a best-dressed beach hut competition – a chance for the lucky few to show off their proud home from home. With so many first-class events taking place offshore, and fantastic views to boot, beach huts are hot property. A dilapidated beach hut of just 12ft by 12ft recently sold for £39,500, a figure double the annual wage of most local people. Beach towns on Lleyn are among the most fashionable in Britain.

PORTH YSGO

Beyond Abersoch, the coastline scenery of Lleyn changes dramatically to an astonishing landscape of ancient, time-worn rocks and boulders. On a sunny summer's day it is another world entirely, far removed from the bright sails and crowded beaches. Just 10 minutes from the road, a walk passes through a valley of ferns and foxgloves, and past a series of small waterfalls, before climbing down wooden steps to a sheltered bay of black gabbro rocks revealed at low tide. Formed from molten magma trapped beneath the earth's surface, these distinctive boulders give Porth Ysgo its otherwordly feel and indeed the area is steeped in legend. The island of Maen Gwenonwy (Gwenonwy's Rock) is named after King Arthur's sister; his last battle is said to have been fought here.

PORTH ALWM

Manganese was mined on the Lleyn peninsula for over a century and nuggets can be found among the distinctive blue-black rocks on the shoreline. Six mines operated intermittently throughout the Victorian age and the first half of the 20th century, with increased production during both world wars. At first, pack mules carried baskets of ore from the mines to the beach, where it was loaded onto small steamships bound for Ellesmere Port, Cheshire. Later, jetties were built and ore was transported from the mines by cable car or rail, parts of which could still be seen on the beaches long after the mines closed down.

ABERDARON *(above and right)*

The whitewashed cottages of Aberdaron cluster beside the wide sand and shingle bay. Pilgrims on their way to Bardsey Island (Ynys Enlli) would depart from this remote fishing village, stopping for food and shelter at the 14th century Y-Gegin Fawr ("the Old Kitchen"). Day visits to the island can still be arranged, setting sail from Aberdaron. The Church of St Hywyn, with twin naves, was built in the 12th century by Gruffydd ap Cynan, King of Gwynedd, and enlarged in 1417. The stone buildings replaced wooden structures, which had been used for worship since the 5th century. It is a sanctuary church where disputes can be settled on the stone chair of peace, and no fugitive can be ejected for 40 days and nights.

ABERDARON BEACH *(above and right)*
The beach can be busy in the summer months, with surfing and sailing enthusiasts making their own pilgrimage to the wide bay. Offshore fishing trips can be organised, with beach fishing popular as well. Annual events, including a regatta with races for all levels and a festival with competitions and concerts, bring hundreds of visitors to the beach. Divers can explore an offshore wreck, known as *The Priscilla*, which sank in the 19th century. Much of the surrounding land is owned by the National Trust, and there are some fine coastal and clifftop walks that thread through gorse and follow in the footsteps of the medieval pilgrims, with superb views of Bardsey Island and the green fields of Lleyn.

UWCHMYNYDD & BARDSEY ISLAND

The headland at the end of the Lleyn peninsula, generally referred to as Uwchmynydd, is the Land's End of North Wales. To get there, walkers pass over open grassland criss-crossed with sheep tracks and scattered with small fields, sheep and heather. The headland's summit, Mynydd Mawr, is a wild spot with magnificent views across the Bardsey Sound, a two-mile wide stretch of water with dangerous tides and currents, to Bardsey Island. So many Christian pilgrims sought sanctuary and were buried on the island that it became known as the Isle of 20,000 Saints and remains of graves can be seen across the island. Dominated by a hill over 500ft (152m) high, Enlli is a now a seabird sanctuary and wildlife refuge with many grey seals.

PORTH LLAWENAN *(right)*

From the rocks at Porth Alwm are views of Porth Llawenan and the rocky headland of Trwyn Talfarach behind. The mountain on the headland, Mynydd Penarfynydd, reaches 580ft (177m) and is owned by the National Trust. Geologically ancient, the headland contains a wide range of rock types. Choughs, the UK's rarest crows, nest in the sea cliffs here and feed in the maritime heath and grassland. Three-quarters of all the UK's choughs nest in Wales as they are attracted to the wild and unspoilt coastlines. Myths tell of King Arthur returning as a chough, and their piercing "chow" call that gave the bird its name can be heard on walks across the Lleyn peninsula.

PORTH DINLLAEN & CARREG DDU

The natural harbour of Porth Dinllaen was almost chosen for development as the main port for ferries to Ireland, but instead this role fell to Holyhead. The long, curving bay is backed by low cliffs. To the western end are clustered fishing cottages of the tiny 18th-century Porth Dinllaen hamlet now owned by the National Trust. The beach is perfect for picnics, walks and bathing, and the red-painted Ty Coch Inn is an ideal place to stop for a bite to eat and a drink. From the promontory at Carreg Ddu are stunning views of the sweeping bay and the mountains of Snowdonia beyond. Seals can often be seen sunning themselves on the rocks here.

LLEYN PENINSULA AT SUNSET

During the daytime, the coast around the Lleyn peninsula is surrounded by golden, sandy coves and vibrant blue waters. The hills are covered with a patchwork of bright green fields and hedgerows. These colours are often transformed as the sun sets to giant red and orange streaked skies above the silvery seas and black silhouettes of headlands and clifftops. The magnificent pinks, yellows and blues in this scene are a reminder of the tranquillity and timelessness of the peninsula. Pilgrims walked for miles under sunsets such as these to reach Bardsey Island, and the sound of waves lapping at the shores and the barks of seals have been heard for centuries.

SOUTH SNOWDONIA

SOUTHERN SNOWDONIA may not have the drama of the high peaks of the Snowdon range but it is packed with mountain scenery and beautiful green valleys. Hikes in this region are refreshingly free of the crowds that flock further north, and begin in remote and secret valleys. The highest peaks in this region, Aran Fawddwy and Penygadair on Cadair Idris, are close to 3,000ft (915m) and steeped in the legend of giants. Views from the Cadair Idris range in particular extend as far as the Lleyn peninsula, with a fine outlook on the picturesque Mawddach estuary. The lakes here are mystical places with glassy blue waters and abundant wildlife. Popular with anglers, they are well-stocked with wild brown and rainbow trout.

LLYNNAU CREGENNEN
In a haunting spot below Cadair Idris and on a plateau beside the Mawddach Estuary lie the Llynnau Cregennen, cradled by hills. The magical lakes are astonishingly photogenic. The area is steeped in history, with ancient standing stones and hut circles. Reached by steep winding roads, visitors flock to the lakes to admire the beautiful mountain scenery and views south to Barmouth and the sea.

ARAN FAWDDWY SUMMIT
To reach the summit of Aran Fawddwy it is a steady climb from the head of a lovely and secret valley. Crowning the highest ridge of southern Snowdonia, the mountain summit is higher than Cadair Idris at 2,976ft (905m). This rewarding view from the rocky plateau takes in the sister peak of Aran Benllyn and to the right, Cwm Croes. Beyond and out of view in this photograph lies Bala Lake (Llyn Tegid), a base for many who hike and climb in the Arans.

ARAN FAWDDWY, THE SUMMIT CAIRN

The stony summit cairn of Aran Fawddwy is said to have been erected by the men of Dinas Mawddwy when they believed Cadair Idris to be 6ft (2m) higher. In fact Aran Fawddwy was found to be 43ft (13m) higher than Penygadair. Both Aran Fawddwy and Aran Benllyn, a mile along the ridge, are associated with Arthurian legends. King Arthur is said to have fought a mighty battle nearby with a giant, Rhita Gawr, who lived on the southern edge of Aran Fawddwy. The giant wished to make a collar for his robe from Arthur's beard. Arthur fought the giant and won, flinging him down the hillside. Aran Benllyn is one of the many places the giant is said to have been buried.

ARAN FAWDDWY

It is a dramatic 1,000ft (305m) drop from the summit of Aran Fawddwy to the lake of Creiglyn Dyfi below. Seen here from Drws Bach, this solitary lake nestles below the towering crags of the ridge. No more than 600ft (183m) across, it is the source of the Afon Dyfi, which flows through Machynlleth to the sea at Aberdyfi and forms a natural boundary between north and south Wales. The river meets Bwlch y Groes (Pass of the Cross), the highest road in North Wales. Passing through a wild and barren landscape travellers discovered a cross at its highest point – a chance to "thank God" for having completed the climb. Today a wooden cross stands where the road meets the turning point for Lake Vyrnwy (Llyn Efyrnwy).

CWM CYWARCH, WAUN CAMDDWR AND DRYSGOL

(above and right)

From the valley at Cywarch, the ascent to Aran Fawddwy follows an old peat-cutter's track along the sides of Hengwm. Views back into the beautiful and secret valley look towards the upper reaches of Cwm Cywarch. The summit of Glasgwm and the tarn of Llyn y Fign lie way beyond the crags. To the left of Cwm Cywarch are the lower grassy plateaux of hills to the west. An anticlockwise circular route of Aran Fawddwy returns along the boggy moorland of Waun Camddwr and through a steep, narrow, occasionally tricky gulley alongside overhanging crags, streams and waterfalls. The scenery is wild and good rock climbs can be found here.

CWM CYWARCH (left)

It is likely that hemp was cultivated in Cwm Cywarch, as the name translates as Hemp Valley. Widely grown across Britain during the Middle Ages, hemp was used for textiles, paper, rope and oil production. Farmers were required to grow hemp to supply the navy with fibres for ropes and, in the 1800s, Harlech was a centre for hemp production. Yellow Welsh poppies grow in the peaceful valley and the tussocky landscape is dotted with trees and a number of small farmsteads. There are opportunities for birdwatching here with buzzards often seen circling the cliffs of Craig Cywarch.

HENGWM

The boat-shaped valley of Hengwm is flanked by a long, straight and regular climb along the steep side of the hill, Pen yr Allt Uchaf. It is not strenuous and leads to Drysgol, and further to the Aran ridge. This magnificent scene from the path looks towards great grassy meadows on the slopes leading up to the summit at Gwaun y Llwyni. The dramatic amphitheatre at the valley head is overlooked by Drws Bach.

MEMORIAL CAIRN, DRWS BACH

The Aran ridge begins at Drws Bach, which translates as the "little door" and stands at 2,500ft (762m). Hikes from Cwm Cywarch that climb the side of Cwm Hengwm reach the ridge through this narrow doorway. A memorial cairn stands here, built to honour SAC Michael Robert Aspin of RAF Mountain Rescue, killed by lightning in 1960. Views from the cairn are outstanding, with sharp drops into Cwm Hengwm in front, and a shallower descent behind, with marvellous views of Creiglyn Dyfi and Aran Fawddwy's eastern face.

CWM CYWARCH

Restrictions on climbing in this area are reviewed annually between landowners and the Snowdonia National Park Authority. Walkers are encouraged to keep to the paths, avoid camping and use stiles to cross the many fences and walls. Dogs are not allowed on these remote tracks. While descending from Aran Fawddwy by route of Waun Camddwr and its rocky moorland, there are fences along the way. To the right of this scene is a climb to Glasgwm, reaching 2,556ft (779m). Heading downhill to Cwm Cywarch from here is a dramatic and steep descent.

PENYGADAIR

At 2,929ft (893m), the summit of Cadair Idris – Penygadair – is a few metres lower than south Snowdonia's highest mountain, Aran Fawddwy. But Cadair's open access offers far better views. On an exceptionally clear day, you can see Bardsey Island 40 miles away at the tip of the Lleyn peninsula. In this photograph, views of the Mawddach Estuary and the faded outline of the peninsula can be seen as a fine back-drop to the sheer precipice of the Cadair Idris northern flank.

CADAIR IDRIS SUMMIT

Cadair Idris means the chair of Idris, who may have been Idris Gawr, a Celtic poet and giant of legend who liked to study the stars from his high throne. In one popular story, though it is not a tale exclusive to Cadair Idris, a visitor who spends a night alone on the summit of the mountain will return either as a madman or a poet.

PENYGADAIR

Cyfrwy (The Saddle) reaches 2,660ft (811m) and is the third highest summit along the ridge with dramatic cliffs. When the Victorians discovered the Welsh mountains, Cadair Idris became a popular climb for many tourists on hired ponies with guides. An old lady trekked early each morning to the Penygadair summit hut to serve many grateful visitors cups of tea.

CRAIG CAU & LLYN CAU *(below)*

Llyn Cau is in an almost ideal location for a high
mountain lake: flanked to the south by the pointed
crag of Craig Cau and to the north by the imposing
ridge of Cadair Idris and its peaks. The 18th-century
artist, Richard Wilson, who inspired many including
Turner, painted a magnificent composition of the lake
with an exaggerated precipice and invented landscape
features. The lake is a fine example of a glaciated cwm
with corries, steep eroded sides and morainic debris
at the lake's outflow. Further corrie lakes can be seen
around Cadair Idris. The natural amphitheatre of
Cwm Cau is perhaps the chair of Idris, with obvious
armrests and seat, though Cwm Gadair to the north
of the summit is also a candidate.

CADAIR IDRIS *(right)*

It is just a short scramble among the loose stones
south of Penygadair to this wonderful viewpoint. It is
reached by the Minfford Path, a route to three peaks
that requires energy and fitness and is exceedingly
steep in places. The route follows the rim around
Craig Cau with sheer drops towards Llyn Cau with its
deep green-blue waters and glasslike appearance.
Looking south, the slope down to the valley at Talyllyn
is extremely long. This ridge is one side of the 20km
(12 mile) Bala-Talyllyn fault, the largest land shift in
Wales. The classic U-shaped valley here was carved by
glaciers that exploited the natural weakness of the
fault. Beyond the rift valley of Talyllyn lie the green
humps of Plynlimon mountain.

LLYN EFYRNWY
(Lake Vyrnwy)

Llyn Efyrnwy is a mystical place. Beneath the shimmering waters of this artificial lake lies a village, Llanwddyn, one of many submerged villages throughout Snowdonia. A masonry dam was constructed in 1889 to collect and transport pure waters to Liverpool. The lake and its surrounding habitat are a nature reserve, with heather moorland, farmland and oak and conifer forest providing a home for a huge variety of birds, butterflies and flowers. In dry summers when the water levels drop the ruins of the old town can sometimes be seen.

LLANGOLLEN (above and right)

The picturesque scenery of the River Dee (Afon Dyfrdwy) is seen here from Llangollen's famous and elegant bridge. The town's centrepiece, the bridge was built by Bishop Trevor in 1345 and today carries motor traffic and, during the summer, international visitors and musicians at Llangollen's lively annual International Eisteddfod. Surrounded by hills, and overlooked by the ruins of the 13th-century Castell Dinas Bran, Llangollen is an ideal place for a leisurely and historic walk. Weirs, falls and miniature rapids can all be found along the river, alongside which runs Thomas Telford's historic road from London to Holyhead and the scenic Llangollen Railway. The fine ruins of a 13th-century Cistercian monastery, Valle Crucis Abbey, are also found close by.

LLYN TRAWSFYNYDD

In this, one of the strongholds of the Welsh language, lies the calm lake of Trawsfynydd surrounded by nature trails. Boats can be hired for a day's leisurely fishing – the lake is popular with the angling community and well-stocked with wild brown and rainbow trout. For 28 years Llyn Trawsfynydd supplied the waters for an atomic power station here. The station closed in 1993, but a visitor centre explains how electricity was generated.

LLYN CELYN

At the foot of the Arenig mountains lies Llyn Celyn, a fine lake of over two miles in length. As with Llyn Trawsfynydd, this lake is actually a reservoir, created to control the flow of the River Dee and provide water for Liverpool. Despite vigorous local opposition, the marshy Tryweryn valley was flooded in 1965, along with the old Welsh-speaking village of Capel Celyn. A lakeside chapel commemorates the community and those buried in its drowned graveyard.

LLYNNAU CREGENNEN (above left and right)

The crystal clear blue waters of the Llynnau Cregennen are edged by grassy reeds and small boulders. These two magical lakes lie 750ft (230m) above the Mawddach Estuary in a green and undulating plateau landscape surrounded by heather-clad mountains. The craggy face of Tyrrau Mawr looms imposingly above the waters, and the heights of Cadair Idris lie further beyond. At several points close to the lakes, and especially from the peak of Tyrrau Mawr, there are magnificent views of the Afon Mawddach, Barmouth and the remote Lleyn peninsula. The lakes are stocked with wild brown and rainbow trout, and the serene atmosphere makes this an ideal place to spend a day fishing.

Once privately owned, the lakes were given to the National Trust in 1959 by Major CL Wynne-Jones in memory of his two sons who were both killed in the Second World War. Several groups of prehistoric standing stones can be found among the fields of sheep and in the forest, many in spectacular settings. The stones are thought to be close to a Bronze Age trackway known as Fford Ddu (The Dark Road) whose route from Tywyn eventually found its way to the Cotswolds.

MAWDDACH ESTUARY

Barmouth Bridge is the longest viaduct in Wales and has carried passengers across the Afon Mawddach since 1860. It is much photographed and has been the feature of many picture postcards sent by Barmouth holidaymakers. Those who have admired the view include the poet John Masefield, heard to say that at certain times the estuary was the most beautiful in Europe. The picturesque Mawddach Trail – built on the track of a disused railway – carries walkers and cyclists along the banks of the estuary where two large bird reserves are situated.

LLYN CYNWCH *(above and right)*

Near Llanfachreth and the village of Nannau lies Llyn Cynwch, a favourite location for anglers, since the lake is stocked with trout regularly throughout the fishing season. A long and narrow sheet of water, the lake is tucked away amongst wooded hillsides of larch and oak. Cadair Idris provides a fine background at its southern end. Parts of the well-known Precipice Walk skirt the side of the lake. The walk follows a gentle route around the low hill of Moel Cynwch and leads to a precipice with outstanding views high above the Mawddach Estuary – across to Barmouth and the sea, as well as south to the Cadair Idris massif.

LLANYMAWDDWY

This tiny church stands in the village of Llanymawddwy, a small settlement beside the River Dovey (Afon Dyfi). The village has a tradition of producing giants, one of whom, named Llywelyn Fawr o Fawddwy, is buried in this churchyard. A local information board reports that bones twice the size of human remains were also found nearby and are thought to belong to the giant of Mawddwy (Cawr Mawddwy), who threw a rock from Aran Fawddwy, leaving marks where his fingers held it. This rock can apparently still be seen just up the valley at Ffridd Wenallt.

WEST SNOWDONIA

THE RUGGED Rhinog mountains overlook many of the coastal scenes in west Snowdonia. Geologically ancient, the volcanic rock in this region was carved into distinctive escarpments by the thick ice of glaciers during the last Ice Age. Drovers led packhorses through the passes between them along ancient routes, while bandits who raided lands to the east hid among the secret routes. The dramatic estuary of Traeth Bach is a haven for wildlife in this region. Alongside Harlech castle, it is home to thousands of migrating birds. Near the estuary grew the town of Porthmadog, once a shipbuilding centre and busy port exporting slate from Snowdonia to locations around the world. Today it is a centre for tourism and a respite from the strenuous climbs of nearby peaks.

MOEL-Y-GEST SUMMIT

There are fine panoramic views from the summit of the small rocky mound of Moel-y-Gest. The mountain stands beside Porthmadog, at the edge of the Lleyn peninsula and beside the far-reaching sands of Traeth Bach. Looking inland to the east in this scene are Cnicht and Moelwyn Mawr. To the north are Moel Ddu and Moel Hebog; to the south, the Rhinog mountains.

CWM BYCHAN (left)

The wild and atmospheric beauty of Llyn Cwm Bychan is unmistakeable in this arresting photograph. The lake stands in a peaceful, remote valley and at the foot of the 2,363ft (720m) Rhinog Fawr. Evidence of glaciation is all around, with bedrock underfoot and striated rock boulders strewn across the valley.

BORTH-Y-GEST *(below)*

This quiet fishing village is less than a mile down the river from Porthmadog and sits alongside the Glaslyn Estuary. Quaint cottages line the clean sand and shingle beach and there are fantastic views from the coastal footpath. But in the 19th century, four busy shipyards in Borth-y-Gest's small harbour built carefully crafted masted ships that traded around the world for many years. One brig called *The Fleetwing*, built in 1874, still exists today. Having worked in many trades in the West Indies, the Mediterranean and West Africa, she was sent to the Falkland Islands and is now used as a storage hulk.

AFON GLASLYN ESTUARY

Half a mile from Borth-y-Gest, it is an easy climb to the summit of Moel-y-Gest, from where there are spectacular views across Traeth Bach to Harlech and the Rhinog mountains beyond. It is said that Prince Madog, the son of Owain Gwynedd, set sail from Borth-y-Gest to discover America, 300 years before Christopher Columbus. At low tide, the course of the Afon Glaslyn can be seen, as well as the mainly agricultural land reclaimed from the saltmarsh and mudflats of the estuary. The sands of Traeth Bach are unsafe for bathing because of strong currents and fast incoming tides.

EVENING SUN, MOEL-Y-GEST

The climb to the summit of Moel-y-Gest, just 859ft (262m) above the town of Porthmadog, is not too strenuous and passes the remains of a granite quarry. Though the quarry was closed in the 1920s, the incline used to transport the granite can still be seen. From the top are spectacular views of the surrounding hills and mountains, including Moel Ddu and Moel Hebog seen in the evening sun in this spectacular photograph. The green valley below is scattered with cottages for rent where walkers can enjoy a picturesque and restful base for travels into nearby Snowdonia.

ROCK CRAGS, MOEL-Y-GEST

Though it is just a miniature mountain, Moel-y-Gest has views as impressive as those from many higher and more challenging peaks in the area. From the summit the views up the valley of the Afon Glaslyn towards Cnicht and Moelwyn Mawr are caught beautifully in this early evening shot. Moel-y-Gest also provides rock climbers with a place to practise their skills when the mountains of Snowdonia are not accessible due to snow or bad weather. Its craggy rocks are distinctive and can be seen overlooking Borth-y-Gest, standing at the gateway to the Lleyn peninsula.

THE COB, PORTHMADOG *(below)*

In the early 19th century, an English MP and local landowner, William Alexander Madocks, decided to build a sea wall and embankment across the Glaslyn Estuary, draining and reclaiming the marshy land behind. He expected Porth Dinllaen on the Lleyn peninsula to become the main port for travel to Ireland and planned to develop a town and port to accommodate travellers on their way there. In a spectacular spot, just south of the Moelwyns and Cnicht, work began on a mile-long embankment across the estuary known as The Cob. Completed in 1811, it reclaimed 7,000 acres of land from the river's mudflats.

PORTHMADOG *(left)*

Porthmadog was originally planned to be the lesser of two towns developed on the reclaimed land. Tremadog, with its cobbled square, was a perfect example of 19th-century town planning and was the birthplace of TE Lawrence. The poet Shelley visited often. Later, Madocks established the port known as Portmadoc, which prospered and grew with the successful export of slate around the world. Though originally named Port Madoc after its founder (Madock's port), it has more recently assumed the name Porthmadog in honour of the Welsh Prince Madog.

MUDFLATS, GLASLYN ESTUARY *(above)*

From the south side of The Cob, the wide mudflats of the Glaslyn Estuary are revealed at low tide and stretch into the distance. Before the causeway was constructed, the estuary was said to be the most beautiful in the whole of Wales. Today, it is a haven for migrating birds and wildlife, and can hold up to 1,500 wigeon in the winter as well as smaller numbers of waders and wildfowl such as Canada geese, mallard and teal. Several beaches around the headland have fine golden sands and small coves.

MARSHES, PORTHMADOG *(below)*

The land reclamation and causeway construction in the estuary changed the course of the Afon Glaslyn and sedimentation increased. Sluice gates were fitted in 1821 to prevent the river being inundated by saltwater. During the winter, when the river is at its fullest, much fresh water builds up behind the causeway. The marshes are protected by the North Wales Wildlife Trust and are home to unusual plant species and rare birds.

QUAYSIDE, PORTHMADOG *(above)*

Slate from the mines of Snowdonia was shipped from Porthmadog harbour to destinations such as Hamburg, Cadiz and South America. Porthmadog went into decline in the 1870s with the arrival of the Cambrian railway and the decline of the slate trade and today the town has become a centre for tourism. The old slate sheds that lined the quayside have been replaced with holiday flats, seen here beneath the Rhinog mountains beyond.

FFESTINIOG RAILWAY *(right)*

The Ffestiniog railway was built to carry slate from the mines of Snowdonia to the harbour for shipping. The 13-mile (20km) scenic trip along a narrow gauge railway leaves from the harbour, travels along The Cob and into the mountains as far as Blaenau Ffestiniog.

PORTHMADOG HARBOUR

(above and right)

Fishing boats and pleasure craft now crowd the handsome marina and harbour at Porthmadog, but it was once an industrious place. At its peak in 1873, 116,000 tons of slate were exported from the port. During the 1870s, it is likely that a thousand vessels visited the harbour each year. A maritime museum situated on the old slate wharf traces the town's history and tells the story of Porthmadog's shipbuilders and traders. The last fleet left Porthmadog harbour in 1945. It is a pleasant stroll around the harbour where there is a pub, café and yacht club.

CWM BYCHAN NEAR CAMPSITE
Sheep graze under the shade of a dwarf oak, beside a clump of boulders: evidence of this remote region's ancient past. The bedrock under foot and many rocks strewn across the valley side of Cwm Bychan are remnants of erosion caused by glaciation during the last Ice Age. The ice covering Snowdonia was at its thickest in this region.

CWM BYCHAN WALKS *(right)*
Reached by a single track road from Llanbedr, passing steeply through pleasant woodland, Cwm Bychan is the starting point for walks to the peak of Rhinog Fawr. The road comes to an end at the head of the lake where parking is provided and a farm stands among the trees. Cuckoos can be seen and heard in Cwm Bychan, and feral goats roam here too.

LLYN CWM BYCHAN

Reeds rise from the calm, cold, blue waters of Llyn Cwm Bychan. The lake is scenically scattered with boulders and lies cradled by the rough, craggy peaks of the Rhinog mountains. This magical scene is enhanced by the sense of solitude and remoteness that is to be found throughout the area. Even during the busiest of seasons in Snowdonia, these upland valleys and rugged hills remain silent and relatively undisturbed. Woodland surrounds the lower parts of the valley and buzzards fly by.

ROMAN STEPS EN ROUTE TO RHINOG FAWR

More magical than the valley and lake below, are the Roman Steps that walkers encounter on their way to the summit of Rhinog Fawr. The climb from the lake passes through ancient oak woodland and an increasingly open, rocky landscape before a gap in the rock reveals the steps leading upwards. The route of the steps follows the pass of Bwlch Tyddiad, probably in use in prehistoric times and certainly used by the Romans, who may have laid down some stone slabs to improve the surface. But the Roman Steps were constructed much later: the positioning of the slabs suggests the route was laid down in medieval times by drovers for their packhorses.

CWM BYCHAN

The drystone walls of the valley farm are surrounded by bushy green woodland and rocky boulders. Clouds brood above the rocky escarpment of Clogwyn Pot and, to the right, the crags at the foot of Rhinog Fawr. Between them is Bwlch Tyddiad, through which the Roman Steps pass to Coed y Brenin – the King's forest. Planted by the Forestry Commission in 1922, the forest was named to commemorate George V's Silver Jubilee in 1935. From there a path leads around to the Rhinog National Nature Reserve and the route between the twin Rhinog peaks. Spectacular views can be seen from the head of the pass.

LLYN CWM BYCHAN

Looking southwards from the lake's edge, Llyn Cwm Bychan stands under the shadow of Carreg-y-Saeth, coloured with heather terraces, and shielding views of Rhinog Fawr behind. This region is remote and desolate, and many rugged mounds are unnamed. It is one of the last great wildernesses in Britain, with sightings of sheep and wild goats. In medieval times the Rhinogs were used as protection by outlaws who lived in Ardudwy, the coastal plain between the mountains and the sea. The bandits raided lands to the east and returned on secret routes through the peaks.

CLIP FROM CWM BYCHAN

From the path that leads to the Roman Steps, the view to the north looks across the green valley bottom and towards the triangular peak of Clip. In such a wild location, the ample tree cover is unusual, but makes the area a delightful spot for camping. A long day's hike past Clip leads through fields of sheep and eventually to Llyn Trawsfynydd on the eastern side of the Rhinog range.

CWM BYCHAN

The rocks in this region are the outcrops of one of the oldest known geological rock formations in the world, the Harlech dome. The Ice Age glaciers cut the mountains into a complex pattern of peaks and valleys, and these rugged mounds remain. Small gold mines in the Coed-y-Brenin forest beyond the Roman Steps are evidence of volcanic action in the region's distant past, while copper was extracted by burning peat in a nearby copper mine. Hiking in this region is strenuous – the heather is thigh deep, while horizontal and shattered rocks are prevalent. These ancient boulders are blanketed in lichen and moss and line the lakeshore.

HARLECH CASTLE, EARLY EVENING *(right)*

Built by Edward I in the late 13th century, the commanding castle at Harlech almost grows from the rock on which it stands. Once, the waters of Tremadog Bay lapped the foot of the castle; today the castle, a World Heritage Site, looks over extensive sand dunes that back the wide golden sands of Harlech Beach.

HARLECH MYTHS AND LEGENDS *(below)*

This sculpture by Ivor Roberts-Jones is inspired by one of the Mabinogion legends, Branwen, Daughter of Llyr. Indeed the rock on which Harlech castle was built is known as Branwen's tower. In the story, Branwen, sister of Bendigeidfran, the King of Britain, leaves Harlech to marry the King of Ireland, Matholwch. She bears a son, Gwern, but she is unhappy and made to work in the kitchens. When Bendigeidfran hears news of her treatment a great war ensues. Branwen is rescued but Gwern is killed and the battle is lost with just seven British survivors. The sculpture shows Bendigeidfran's return, bearing the body of Gwern.

TOWN CENTRE

The attractive town of Harlech sits on a ridge behind the castle. Its narrow streets have many breathtaking views. Traditional Welsh stone cottages house cafes, potteries, restaurants, gift shops and art galleries. A quiet market centre for centuries, the town's dependency on tourism grew after the Cambrian Coast Railway was built in 1867.

FAIRBOURNE

Dramatic clouds descend on the mountains that surround the Mawddach Estuary behind the wooden viaduct. The longest railway bridge in Wales, the bridge is more than 125 years old and still used. It carries trains on the Cambrian Coast line, and has a pedestrian walkway for those who would prefer to take their time and admire the views. From Fairbourne, at the other end of the viaduct from the bustle of Barmouth, is a miniature steam railway where visitors can take locomotives on a circular route with views of the sea and estuary. The line was originally constructed for the transportation of stone for the abutments of the Barmouth Railway Bridge. Visitors can return to Barmouth by ferry across the bay.

MAWDDACH ESTUARY FROM PRECIPICE WALK

A circular two-mile route known as the Precipice Walk has incomparable views of the Mawddach Estuary and Llyn Cynwch, as well as views south to Cadair Idris. The estuary runs nine miles inland to Dolgellau and its beauty has been the inspiration for many artists and writers. Turner painted scenes here and Wordsworth described the estuary as "sublime" and comparable to the finest in Scotland. Much of Charles Darwin's *The Descent of Man* was written in a house overlooking the estuary, whilst John Ruskin said that the only journey in the world that had views to compare with the one from Dolgellau to Barmouth, was the journey from Barmouth to Dolgellau.

GALLT-YR-OGOF & TRYFAN

To the south of the A5, between Bethesda and Capel Curig lies Tryfan ("the Trident"),
one of the most easily recognisable peaks of North Snowdonia. In this photograph,
the distinctive shark's fin outline of the mountain can be seen looming behind Gallt-
yr-Ogof in the foreground. Although Tryfan is only 3,010ft (917m), it is one of the
most challenging summits in North Wales and is where the first successful
expedition to Everest trained in the early 1950s.